Draw Along With Tidy Tim

The 'Get to Know Me' series is made up of resources aimed at children with additional needs. Developed by child psychologist Dr Louise Lightfoot and illustrated by Catherine Hicks, the series includes activities specific to anxiety, depression and Obsessive Compulsive Disorder (OCD). This book, *Draw Along With Tidy Tim*, is an activity-based picture book story, in which individual children are encouraged to interact with the story in a creative way – through writing, drawing, scrap booking, collage, activities etc.

Active engagement helps children to understand and process information, and aids long-term recall. It has been designed to support the individual child and encourage an empathetic and inclusive environment. In this book, we meet Tidy Tim, an octopus with many arms but not many friends. His swirly whirly feelings make him spend all day cleaning and tidying his house instead of going out and making friends. But one day, Tidy Tim gets himself into a terrible tangle and realises he needs the help of Jenni the Jellyfish, who helps him untangle his arms and his feelings.

This book was written with children with OCD in mind, providing an opportunity to relate to Tim's thoughts, feelings, behaviours and experiences. However, children with a range of needs may benefit from the story. The book is written in a narrative style, so it does not use diagnostic labels and is not intended for this purpose. Instead the focus is on creating a common language which children can understand and use to make sense of how they are feeling.

A practitioner guidebook is also available (ISBN 978-0-8153-4948-8).

Dr Louise Lightfoot is an Educational and Child Psychologist working with children and young people aged 0–25. She holds a BA in Educational Studies, MEd in the Psychology of Education and doctorate in Educational and Child Psychology. Louise has worked in a variety of settings ranging from mainstream schools to secure units and psychiatric facilities, and has a special interest in working to empower at risk or 'hard to reach' groups. As a person who suffers with Ehlers Danlos, stroke and dyslexia, she has a first-hand understanding of the frustrations and difficulties that accompany a specific physical or learning difficulty. Louise currently works as an HCPC registered Independent Psychologist. If you would like to discuss working with her, please contact Louise at: louise.lightfoot@hotmail.co.uk

Catherine Hicks is an East Yorkshire artist, illustrator, wife and mother. She spent 13 years as a Registered Veterinary Nurse before injury and chronic illnesses led to her creative hobby becoming therapy. When Catherine and Louise were introduced, it was obvious they were kindred spirits and from there the Get to Know Me Series was born.

GET TO KNOW ME SERIES

Series author: Dr Louise Lightfoot
Illustrated by: Catherine Hicks

The **'Get to Know Me'** series is a series of resources aimed at children with SEN or EBD and the professionals who support them in the mainstream primary classroom. Each resource concentrates on a different condition and comprises of three titles, available separately.

A **traditional children's picture book** – designed to support the individual child but also to be used in whole class teaching, to encourage an empathetic and inclusive environment.

An **interactive workbook**. This is a workbook version of the story in which individual children are encouraged to interact with the story in a creative way – through writing, drawing, scrap booking, collage, activities etc. (templates and cut outs will be made available online). Children are more likely to understand and process information if they have had to actively engage with it. The workbook will aid long-term recall and increase the level of understanding.

A **practitioner guide** created for key adults (teachers, therapists and parents) by a child psychologist, with activities specific to each condition. These activities will link to the books and offer practical tools and strategies to support the child and those around them in addition to the information specific to the condition to improve understanding of a child's needs to promote empathy and acceptance.

https://www.routledge.com/Get-To-Know-Me/book-series/GKM

Books included in this series:

Set 1 Get to Know Me: Anxiety
Available as a set and individual books

Book 1
Supporting Children with Anxiety to Understand and Celebrate Difference
A Get to Know Me Workbook and Guide for Parents and Practitioners
PB 978-0-8153-4941-9
eBook 978-1-351-16492-4

Book 2
Sammy Sloth
Get to Know Me: Anxiety
PB 978-0-8153-4953-2
eBook 978-1-351-16452-8

Book 3
Draw Along With Sammy Sloth
Get to Know Me: Anxiety
PB 978-0-8153-4942-6
eBook 978-1-351-16484-9

Set 2 Get to Know Me: Depression
Available as a set and individual books

Book 1
Supporting Children with Depression to Understand and Celebrate Difference
A Get to Know Me Workbook and Guide for Parents and Practitioners
PB 978-0-8153-4943-3
eBook 978-1-351-16480-1

Book 2
Silver Matilda
Get to Know Me: Depression
PB 978-0-8153-4945-7
eBook 978-1-351-16476-4

Book 3
Draw Along With Silver Matilda
Get to Know Me: Depression
PB 978-0-8153-4946-4
eBook 978-1-351-16472-6

Set 3 Get to Know Me: OCD
Available as a set and individual books

Book 1
Supporting Children with OCD to Understand and Celebrate Difference
A Get to Know Me Workbook and Guide for Parents and Practitioners
PB 978-0-8153-4948-8
eBook 978-1-351-16468-9

Book 2
Tidy Tim
Get to Know Me: OCD
PB 978-0-8153-4950-1
eBook 978-1-351-16460-3

Book 3
Draw Along With Tidy Tim
Get to Know Me: OCD
PB 978-0-8153-4951-8
eBook 978-1-351-16456-6

DRAW
ALONG WITH TIDY TIM

GET TO KNOW ME: OCD

DRAW YOUR OWN PICTURES FOR THE TIDY TIM STORY

DR LOUISE LIGHTFOOT

ILLUSTRATED BY CATHERINE HICKS

 Routledge
Taylor & Francis Group

LONDON AND NEW YORK

First published 2020
by Routledge
2 Park Square, Milton Park, Abingdon, Oxon OX14 4RN

and by Routledge
52 Vanderbilt Avenue, New York, NY 10017

Routledge is an imprint of the Taylor & Francis Group, an informa business

British Library Cataloguing-in-Publication Data
A catalogue record for this book is available from the British Library

Library of Congress Cataloging-in-Publication Data
A catalog record for this book has been requested

ISBN: 978-0-8153-4951-8 (pbk)
ISBN: 978-1-351-16456-6 (ebk)

Typeset in Stone Informal
by Apex CoVantage, LLC

CONTENTS

WORK BOOK INSTRUCTIONS FOR PRACTITIONERS, PARENTS AND CARERS

The work book or draw along booklet can be useful in engaging children with poor literacy or a perceived dislike of formal 'work'. Often students with poor literacy, or those who struggle with comprehension, are not readily engaged in stories that may be of therapeutic value to them. Some children appear to read well but, without additional prompts, may not understand the story or how it may relate to others/themselves. Often children will read with a focus on speed rather than on understanding and will look to the pictures for information when asked questions about what they have just read.

In taking away the pictures, this forces children to be active in their engagement with the story itself as they cannot rely on images to support their understanding. By asking pupils to draw (or colour pre-drawn images dependent on ability) images that correspond to the given text, this not only consolidates their understanding of the story but helps to engage the child in a creative process. Some children are more readily engaged in a task in which they can take ownership due their participation. They are able to create their own book which can represent their abilities when applied, highlight any specific skills and act as a reminder of what they can achieve, especially if this surpasses their own expectations.

The booklet should be read with the support of a suitably skilled adult who has an understanding of the child's literacy abilities. If the child is able to read the story they should be encouraged to do so and to draw on each page a corresponding image. For able or confident pupils, they may be able to draw the complete image using pens/crayons complete with facial features depicting the mood and tone of the scene. Others may need more support and may colour, cut and stick in pre-drawn images and draw facial expressions with prompting from an adult or through choosing a facial expression from a given selection. Some children may be hesitant to draw but have great ideas and may ask an adult to draw their vision or use a computer to search for suitable images. However the book is completed, what matters is that all work is child-led and that their work is treated in a non-judgemental and positive manner. The adult should reassure the child that there is no right or wrong way to approach the task

The adult should gauge how appropriate it is to use the follow up questions provided (this may depend on verbal skills, confidence and trust/rapport) and, if appropriate, the adult may decide to explore in depth a particular section of the story, for example 'asking for help' if this is pertinent to the child's behaviour. In such a case they may decide to use the provided activities that are linked to each section of the story. An older or more able child might go through the book drawing each picture, discussing relevant topics and completing every additional activity. For some children, this process may be too much emotionally/beyond their attention span. The length of each session, the adult chosen to support the child, and timing of the session are all factors that will contribute to the success of the work.

Adults engaging in such work should be suitably supported. Best practice is to offer supervision to them by an appropriate adult in recognition of the emotionally challenging nature of this delicate and potentially stressful work. Adults are encouraged to reflect on each session and to note useful insights; for example, can the child infer the characters emotions during a scene? Can they represent this through facial expression? Body language? Use of colour? How can any such observations be supported in the future?

The child is able to keep/refer back to their book and should be encouraged to take ownership of it in order to encourage engagement and improve self-esteem.

Deep, deep down in the ocean
Where squishy fishes swim,
Lived many different creatures
And an octopus called Tim.

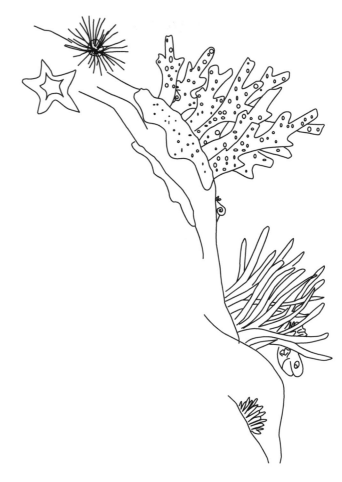

QUESTIONS: Can you draw Tim with his friends?
Or find his picture at the back of this book and colour it, cut it out and stick it at the back of the book?

Tim wasn't very friendly
Or blessed with many charms,
But Tim had lots of other skills
As well as lots of arms.

QUESTION: Tim is always busy. What keeps you busy? Name one thing you like to do.

Tim was super organised
And always had a plan;
His house was very ordered
And always spick and span.

QUESTIONS: *What does your bedroom look like?*
Draw a picture of it, are you as Tidy
as Tidy Tim?

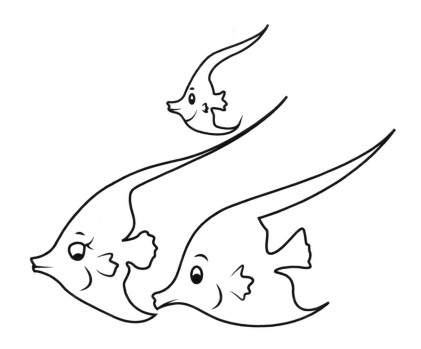

One day a knock came to his door,
He heard a small voice say,
"Hello, Tim – are you in there?
Oh, won't you come and play?"

He looked out of his window
"It's me," a voice declared.
"It's Jenni the jelly fish! Please come play!"
But Tim just stood and stared.

ACTIVITY: Draw, talk or write about someone who asks you to play.

"I'm busy," Tim replied at once
"I've lots of things to do
The house is very messy
I have no time for you"

Jenni asked Tim every day,
Though he never once came out
She'd ask him still, just in case,
And so he wouldn't feel left out.

*QUESTION: What distracts you? Draw a picture or cut
and stick pictures of things that also distract Tim.*

Jenni turned and swam away
And Tim felt sad and mean,
But then the buzzing built inside
And Tim began to clean.

QUESTIONS: *Would you have gone to play with Jenni, or stayed to clean the house? What do you think?*

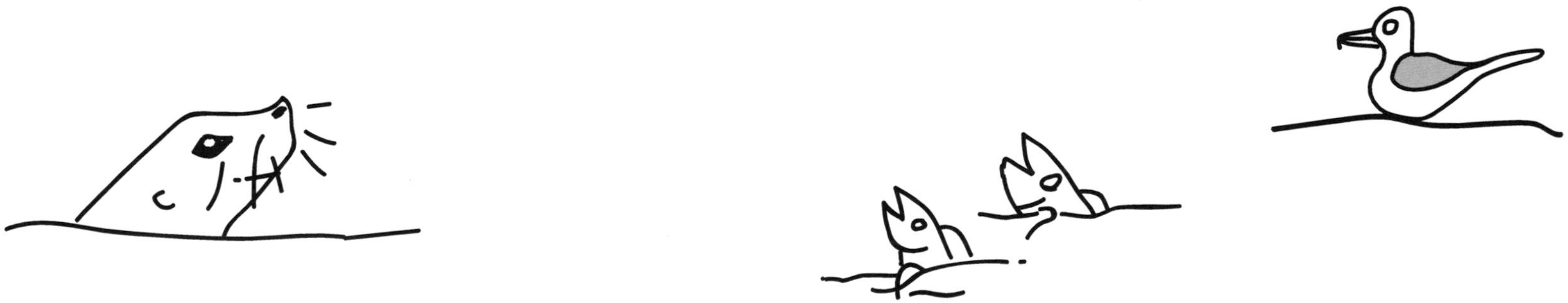

The swirling feelings grew inside
his arms began to whiz,
He rushed and raced about the house
In a swirly twirly tiz.

QUESTION: How do you think Tim feels? Draw, discuss or write about it.

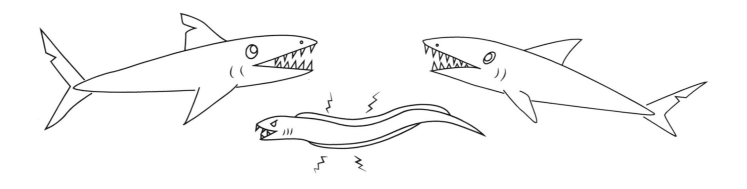

He used his arms to wash and mop
And squish and splash and jangle;
But Tim was such a whirlwind
It ended in a tangle.

*QUESTION: How would you help Tim? Draw, discuss or
write about it.*

His arms were in a muddle
Poor Tim let out a groan.
He'd tied himself all up in knots
And he was all alone.

QUESTION: What makes Tim muddled?
Draw or discuss it.

He wriggled and he squiggled
And then let out a yelp;
He'd only made it worse
He knew he needed help.

QUESTION: How could you help Tim? Draw, write or discuss your ideas.

He couldn't fix this by himself
No matter how he tried,
He'd need a friend to help him
He'd have to go outside.

QUESTION: What does your 'outside' look like?
Draw, write or discuss it.

Tim found Jenni playing,
She helped him right away.
"I'll help," she said, "with one request,
That afterwards you play."

QUESTION: How have your friends helped you? Draw, write or discuss this.

"But everything's a mess," said Tim,
"I can't forget it's there."
"Well, how about we don't," she said,
"But right now let's not care.

QUESTION: What helps you forget and have fun? Draw, write or discuss this.

"Let's just play together
Let's splash and play about;
And then when playtime's over
We'll go and sort it out.

QUESTION: *Do you like to play with your friends? Draw or write about it.*

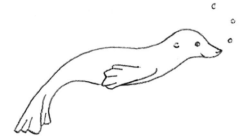

"And I can come and help you
That's if you want a friend;
My arms may not be as fast like yours
But mine are yours to lend.

"I might not be efficient
Or I might not be as strong;
But if we work together
It might not take as long.

ACTIVITY: Draw (or colour, cut and stick) a time when working with someone else made it easier than working alone.

"And if you want to carry on
And do things your own way,
I'll still pop by and think of you
And ask you out to out to play"

"And you can always call me
If you're ever in a muddle,
And I'll be there to help you out
And offer you a cuddle."

ACTIVITY: Draw some more sea creatures playing.

With Jenni as his trusted friend
And her accepting him,
He saw what made him different
Also made him Tim!!

ACTIVITY: Draw what makes you happy!

The tizzy feelings faded
As he realised, in the end,
He did not need more arms,
What he needed was a friend

QUESTION: Do you have a special friend? Draw your friend.

Colour, cut and stick pictures – use these however you like!

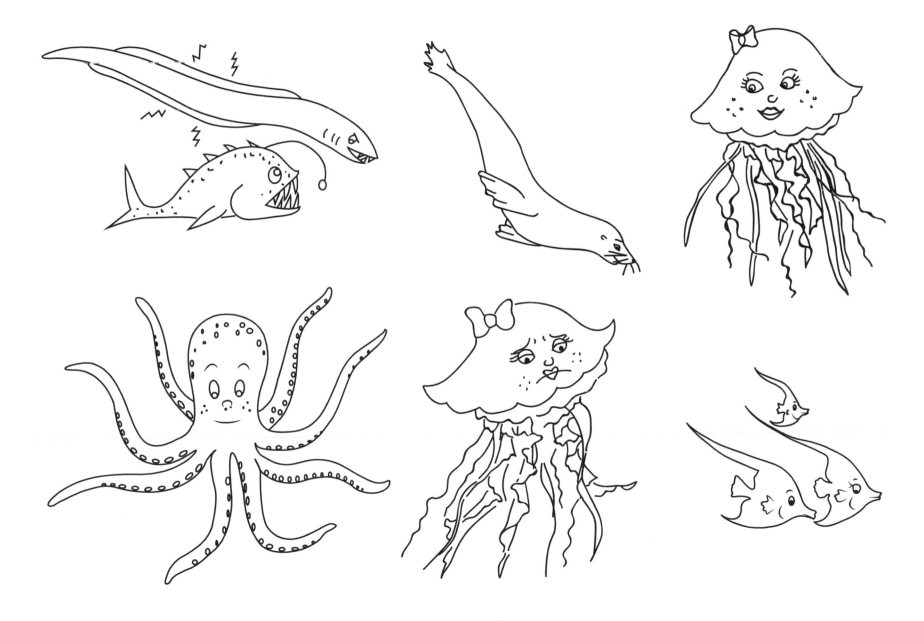